CHOICE OF GUITAR

If you wish to play Pop, Folk, Blues or Plectrum Guitar, a steel string guitar would be most suitable for your needs.

The neck on this guitar will be fairly narrow and as a result you may find difficulty in placing your fingers of the left hand on to the strings without touching those on either side. This is a common difficulty with beginners. Also, with the steel strings, you may find that the tops of your fingers become sore. However, after a short time these difficulties will present no problem.

If, on the other hand, you wish to play fingerstyle or classical guitar, it would be advisable to purchase a Spanish guitar which has a wider fingerboard plus nylon strings which are easier on the fingers.

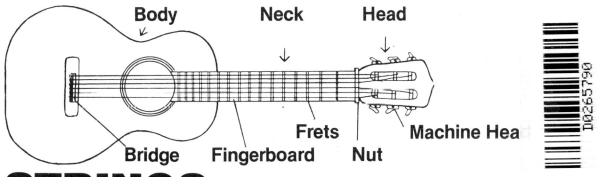

Body   Neck   Head

Frets   Machine Hea[d]

Bridge   Fingerboard   Nut

STRINGS

In order to bring out the best results in your playing and a better sound from your guitar, you should change your strings regularly. There is no hard or fast rule for this as it depends on how much use they are given.

Most pupils do not notice how the strings are wearing out with a resulting deterioration in sound, until they start to unravel and only make a noise.

A concert guitarist may change his strings about once a week, or indeed, he may change them before each performance. But for the average player the strings should be replaced approximately every three or four months.

When buying strings you should get the best you can afford. Remember there is not a great difference in price between a top quality set and an inferior set. But the top quality ones will sound better, last longer, and give you more playing satisfaction.

Before playing always make sure your hands are clean and free from perspiration as otherwise the quality of sound from the strings will be impaired.

NAILS

The nails on your left hand should be kept as short as possible so that you may press the strings down firmly and cleanly on to the fingerboard.

In order that you may play fingerstyle the nails on your right hand should extend slightly above the fingertips.

If your nails are anyway soft and you want them to remain at the proper length you should apply approximately six coatings of colourless nail lacquer with a short interval between each application to allow for drying.

If you have steel strings on your guitar they will wear the nails down very quickly so it is best to purchase a set of finger picks and a thumb pick.
I personally, have always found the finger picks awkward to play with as you can only pick in one direction with them. The thumb pick, however, presents no problem and is quite easily managed.

HOLDING THE GUITAR

Playing Position: It is best to sit on an upright chair as you may find it awkward trying to avoid the arms on an armchair. Also when sitting, cross one leg over the other to add height to the guitar.

Right Hand Position: Look carefully at right hand in diagram. Notice that the hand is arched and dipped down slightly while the thumb remains clear of the fingers. This is very important as it enables you to pluck up with full width of nail and strum down clearly.

Left Hand Position: Notice the left hand is nicely curved from the tip of the fingers to the back of the wrist while the thumb is pressed against the back of the fingerboard.

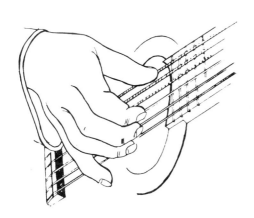

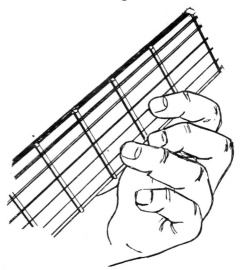

Being a beginner you may find difficulty in positioning the fingers in the proper chord shapes. You should correct this at once by making sure your fingers, wrist and shoulders are relaxed.

TUNING THE GUITAR

Before beginning to play the guitar you must learn how to tune it. Steel strings will remain in tune for a considerable length of time but nylon ones lose their tension more easily (often due to changes in temperature).

You can tune your guitar in the three following ways:

PIANO

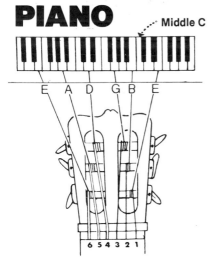

Middle C

E A D G B E

6 5 4 3 2 1

PITCH PIPES

This is perhaps the best way to tune your guitar accurately if you do not have a piano. Each pipe has the name of the string marked on it. Blow gently into the pipe and tune the corresponding string until both strings and pipe produce the same sound.

For the pipe with D stamped on it you would tune the D or fourth string etc. Do not forget there are two E strings on the guitar and the thin one will sound much higher than the thick one which will give the lowest sound on the pitch pipe.

RELATIVE TUNING

This is perhaps the hardest way to tune the guitar but once learned it is the best way as you do not have to depend on piano or pitch pipes etc.

1. Tune the E or sixth string which is the thickest one to where it is not too taut or too loose.
2. Press the E or sixth string just before the fifth fret and tune the A or fifth string till it produces the same sound.
3. Press the A or fifth string just behind the fifth fret and tune the D or fourth string.
4. Press the D or fourth string just behind the fifth fret and tune the G or third string.
5. Press the G or third string just behind the fourth fret and tune the B or second string.
6. Press the B or second string just behind the fifth fret and tune the E or first string.

Lesson 3

HOW TO READ CHORD DIAGRAMS

The vertical lines represent the strings and the horizontal lines represent the frets.

Place your first finger on the E or 1st string, which is the thinnest one, inside the first fret.

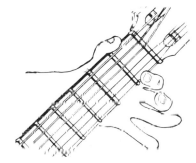

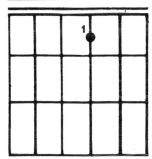

Place your first finger on the G or 3rd string, inside the first fret.

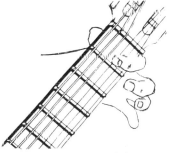

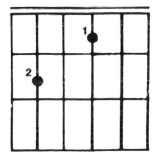

Place your first finger on the G or 3rd string inside the first fret, then place your second finger Inside the second fret on the A or 5th string.

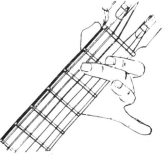

MAJOR CHORDS
IN THE KEY OF 'A'

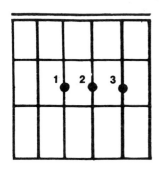 A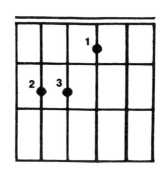

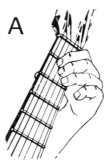 E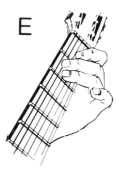

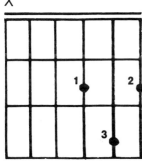 D

Practise these chords carefully.
Before beginning you should
read the following paragraph.

(Don't play 6th string on D chord.)

When you have become accustomed to a chord shape, practise placing your
fingers into the chord shape and releasing immediately, then place your fingers
back into the chord shape as quickly as possible and release again. Continue in
this manner for as long as possible. This will help build up speed in playing.

As you become more familiar with the chords it is essential that you should
learn to play them without looking at your fingers.

Practise this exercise carefully. Strum the given chord three times before
changing to the next.

A \\\ |E \\\ |A\\\ |E \\\ |A\\\ |D\\\ |A\\\ |D\\\ |E\\\ |D\\\ |E\\\

If you repeat this exercise constantly you should have no trouble in changing
from one chord to another.

Change chords where indicated. The chords are written immediately
underneath the words.

SILENT NIGHT

Silent night, Holy night, all is calm, all is bright,
A   E   A
Round yon Virgin Mother and Child,
D   A
Holy Infant so tender and mild,
D   A
Sleep in heavenly peace, sleep in heavenly peace
E   A   E   A

MAJOR CHORDS
IN THE KEY OF 'C'

These chords are a little more difficult than those in the last lesson, especially the chord of F. With a little practise you should master them quite swiftly.

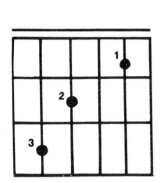

C

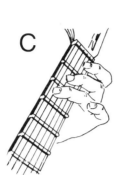

X

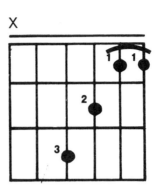

F

PRESS DOWN
FIRMLY

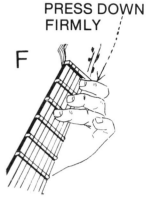

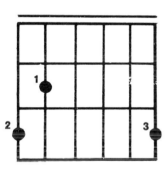

G

The following tunes are played in waltz rhythm.

COCKLES AND MUSSELS

In Dublin's fair city where the girls are so pretty
  C   G7

I first set my eyes on sweet Molly Malone
  C   G

She wheels her wheelbarrow through streets broad and narrow,
    C   G7

Crying cockles and mussels alive-alive-o.
    C   G7   C

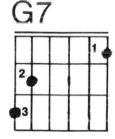

G7

MY DARLING CLEMENTINE

Oh my darling oh my darling oh my darling Clementine
    C   G

You are lost and gone forever, dreadful sorry Clementine
    F   C   G7   C

STRUMMING THE GUITAR

When strumming down on the strings or plucking up always use the full width of your nails.

STRUM 1

Here is a very effective strumming technique which can be used for many songs and is very common in country and western music.

Hold chord of C

1. Hit down with your first finger or plectrum on the fifth and sixth strings.
2. Hit down with the same finger on the first three strings.
3. Bring your finger back on the same three strings.

The rhythm will be one, two and, one, two and etc.
   The following gives some indication of the beat:-
Dom-Dicka, Dom-Dicka etc.
   The following tunes can be played to this rhythm:-

THE BANKS OF THE OHIO

I asked my love to take a walk
       C   G7
To take a walk, just a little walk
    F   C
Down be-side where the waters flow
     Em   F
Down by the banks of the Ohi-o
       C   G7   C
And only say that you'll be mine
      C   G7
In no other arms en-twine
   F   C
Down be-side where the waters flow
     Em   F
Down by the banks of the Ohio
     C   G7   C

I held a knife against her breast
As into my arms she pressed
She cried, Oh! Willie, don't murder me,
I'm not prepared for eternity.

I started home 'tween twelve and one
I cried, My God, what have I done,
Killed the only woman I loved
Because she would not be my bride.

And only say that you'll, etc.

Use these fingerings of C and F for The Banks of the Ohio:

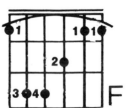

C

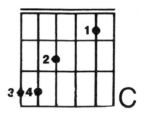

F

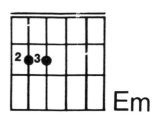

Em

RED RIVER VALLEY

Strike the fifth and fourth bass strings for the D chord.

From the valley they say you are going
       G

We will miss your bright eyes and sweet smile
                              D

For they say you are taking the sunshine
       G   C

That brightens our pathways awhile
     D   G

Lesson 7

STRUM 2

This strum is similar to the previous one in that the rhythm is the same, and it can be used for the same tunes.

Play chord of C. Use your thumb and first finger, or plectrum.

1. Hit the fifth string with the thumb.
2. Hit down on the first three strings with your first finger.
3. Bring your first finger back up on the same three strings.

This should be played with a free flowing movement.
Strike the sixth bass string for the G7 and F chords.
Strike the fourth bass string for the D chord.

THE SAINTS

Oh when the saints, oh when the saints,
                 C

Oh when the saints go marching in
                             G7

I want to be in that num-ber
           C   F

When the saints go mar-ching in
      C   G7   C

DOWN BY THE RIVERSIDE

Well I met my little bright eyed doll, down by the riverside
     G

Down by the riverside, down by the riverside
D   G

Well I met my little bright eyed doll, down by the riverside

Down by the riverside
D   G

Well I kissed my little bright eyed doll, down by the riverside etc.

Well I wed my little bright eyed doll, down by the riverside etc.

STRUM 3

This method of strumming can be used for songs with a waltz rhythm which is one two three, one two three etc.

Play chord of G. Use your first finger or plectrum.

1. Hit down on the fifth and sixth strings only.
2. Hit down on the first three strings.
3. Bring your finger back on the same three strings.
4. Hit back down on the first three strings.
5. Bring your finger back up the same three strings.
You will have played — Down, Down up-Down up, Down, Down up-Down up etc. and it will sound like Dom-Dicka-Dicka, Dom-Dicka-Dicka etc.
    You may play the following tunes in the same rhythm:-
Strike the fifth and fourth bass strings for the D and D7 chords.

MY BONNIE

My bonnie lies over the ocean
    G   C   G
My bonnie lies over the sea
                          D
My bonnie lies over the ocean
    G   C   G
Oh bring back my bonnie to me
      C   D7   G

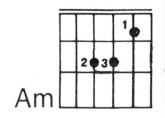

D7

CHORUS

Bring back, bring back,
  G   C   Am
Bring back my bonnie to me to me
D7   G
Bring back oh bring back,
             C   Am
Oh bring back my bonnie to me
    D7   G

Am

ON TOP OF OLD SMOKY

On top of Old Smoky all covered with snow
    G   C   G
I lost my true lover from courtin' too slow
               D   G
For courtin's a pleasure and parting is grief
              C   G
And a false hearted lover is worse than a thief
             D   G

FINGERSTYLES

Some tunes may not be suitable for strumming and will sound better when played with an appropriate fingerstyle.

When playing fingerstyle, the first finger normally plucks the third string, the second finger the second string and the third finger the first string. The thumb may alternate on the fourth, fifth and sixth strings.

FINGERSTYLE 1

Here is a waltz rhythm fingerstyle for accompanying slow tunes. Although the tune may be slow this arpeggio should be played moderately fast.

Play chord of C

1. Press the thumb down on the fifth string.
2. Pluck the third string with the first finger.
3. Pluck the second string with the second finger.
4. Pluck the first string with the third finger.
5. Pluck the second string with the second finger.
6. Pluck the third string with the first finger.

The rhythm will be 1 and, 2and, 3 and.

Strike the sixth bass string for the E, G, G7 and F chords.
Strike the fourth bass string for the D and D7 chords.

AMAZING GRACE

Amazing grace how sweet the sound
    C   C7   F   C
That saved a wretch like me
              Em   G
I once was lost but now am found
 C   C7   F   C
Was blind but now I see.
            G7   C

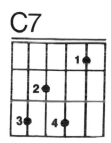

C7

PLAISIR D'AMOUR (THE JOYS OF LOVE)

The joys of love are but a moment long
   G   D G   C   G   D
The pain of love en-dures the whole night long
   C D G   C   G   D G
Your eyes kissed mine I saw a love in them shine
   G   D   G   C   G   D
You brought me heaven on earth when your eyes kissed mine
   C   D7 G   C   G   D G

My love loves me and all the wonders I see
A rainbow shines in my window my love loves me

And now she is gone like a dream that fades into the dawn
This world stays locked in my heart strings my love loves me

FINGERSTYLE 2

This fingerstyle may be used in tunes that are slow but remain at a steady pace
1234, 1234, etc.

Play chord of D

1. Pluck the fourth string with the thumb.
2. Pluck the third string with the first finger.
3. Pluck the second string with the second finger.
4. Pluck the first string with the third finger.

You may also play the above sequence 1 2 4 3. Play the following tunes in both ways.
Strike the fifth bass string for the A, A7, and Am chords.
Strike the sixth bass string for the G chord.

SLOOP JOHN B

We sailed on the sloop John B.
     D
My grandpappy and me

Round the seven seas we did roam
               A
Drinking all night got into a fight
        D   G
I feel so broke up I wanna go home
 D   A7   D

CHORUS

So hoist up the John B's sails
    D
See how the mainsail sets

Call for the captain ashore, let me go home
                  A
I wanna go home, I wanna go home
         D   G
I feel so broke up I wanna go home
 D   A7   D

The captain's a wicked man,
He gets drunk whenever he can
He don't give a damn about grandpappy and me
He kicks us around and shoves us about
I feel so broke up I wanna go home.

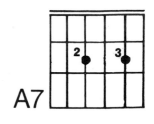

A7

FINGERSTYLES

Here is a fingerstyle to play Scarborough Fair or a similar tune in the waltz rhythm.

Play chord of Am
1. Play the fifth string with the thumb.
2. Pluck the first string with the third finger.
3. Pluck the third string with the first finger.
4. Pluck the second string with the second finger.
5. Play the fourth string with the thumb.
6. Pluck the third string with the first finger.

The rhythm is like fingerstyle 1: one and, two and, three and.
Strike the fifth and fourth bass strings for the Am and C chords.
Strike the sixth and fourth bass strings for the G and Em chords.
Strike the fourth bass string twice for the D chord.

SCARBOROUGH FAIR

Are you going to Scar-borough Fair,
Am   G   Am
Parsley, sage, rose-ma-ry and thyme,
                 D   Am
Remember me to one who lives there
Am   C   G
For she once was a true love of mine
     Am   G   Am

Tell her to make me a cambric shirt,
Parsley, sage rose-ma-ry and thyme
Without no seams or fine needle work
Then she'll be a true love of mine

Tell her to find me an acre of land
Parsley, sage, rosemary and thyme
Between the salt water and the sea strand
Then she'll be a true love of mine

AULD LANG SYNE

Should auld acquaintance be forgot and never brought to mind
     G   Em   Am   D7   G   Em   C
Should auld acquaintance be forgot and days of auld Lang Syne
     G   Em   Am   D7   C   Am   G
For auld Lang-Syne my dear for auld Lang Syne
   G   Em   Am   D7   G   Em C
We'll take a cup o'kindness dear for auld Lang Syne
     G   Em   Am   D7   C   Am G

FINGERSTYLE 4

(Double Thumbing)

This is a very effective way of accompanying songs. It should be played as quickly as possible to achieve the desired result.

Play chord of A

1. Play the fifth string with the thumb.
2. Pluck the first string immediately with the second finger.
3. Play the fourth string with the thumb.
4. Pluck the second string immediately with the first finger.

The rhythm is one and two and, one and two and, etc. and will sound like Doma-Loma-Doma-Loma etc.
Learn this fingerstyle well and when you can play it with sufficient ease, you may, if you wish, alternate on other strings using the same basic style.
Here are tunes which are suited to double thumbing.

Strike the fourth and third strings with the thumb for the D chord.
Strike the sixth and fourth strings for the E chord.

OLD McDONALD HAD A FARM

Old McDonald had a farm E-I-E-I-O
A   D   A   E A
And on that farm he had a duck E-I-E-I-O
                    D   A   E A
With a quack, quack, here and a quack, quack there,
  A
Here a quack there a quack everywhere a quack, quack,
Old McDonald had a farm E-I-E-I-O
                 D   A   E A

SHE'LL BE COMING ROUND THE MOUNTAIN

She'll be coming round the mountain when she comes
        A
She'll be coming round the mountain when she comes
                                   E
She'll be coming round the mountain, coming round the mountain
        A   D
She'll be coming round the mountain when she comes
     A   E   A

She'll be driving six white horses when she comes etc.

She'll be wearing a blue bonnet when she comes etc.

Oh we'll all go out to meet her when she comes etc.

FINGERSTYLE
(Clawhammer)

The clawhammer is the style most commonly used by experienced guitarists. It is quite difficult to learn but once mastered its effective sound proves well worth the effort.

Play chord of G

1. Pluck the sixth string with the thumb and at the same time pluck the first string with the second finger.
2. Pluck the third string with the thumb.
3. Pluck the second string with the first finger.
4. Pluck the sixth string with the thumb.
5. Pluck the first string with the second finger.
6. Pluck the third string with the thumb.
   The rhythm is counted one, two and, three and, four.
   It is important to practise this fingerstyle thoroughly before attempting to play the following tunes.

Strike the sixth and third strings with the thumb for the G, Em, F and G7 chords.
Strike the fifth and third strings with the thumb for the C and C7 chords.
Strike the fourth and third strings with the thumb for the D, D7 and Dm chords.

THE YELLOW ROSE OF TEXAS

Oh the yellow rose of Texas the girl I long to see
     G   Em
No one could ever love her not half as much as me
    C   G   D
You can sing about your Clementine
       G
Or speak of Rosy Lee
          Em
But the yellow rose of Texas is the only girl for me
      C   D7   G

OLD FOLKS AT HOME

Way down upon the Swanee river
C   C7   F
Far, far a-way
C   Em   G7
That's where my heart is turning ever
C   C7   F
There's where the old folks stay
C   Em   Dm   G7 C
All the world is sad and dreary everywhere I roam
G7   C   F   C
Oh darkies how my heart grows weary far from the old folks at home
  C7   F   C Em   Dm G7   C

Dm

BAR CHORDS

This is a method of placing your first finger across the full width of the strings thereby enabling you to play chords in any position.

Before learning how to get the different chords it is necessary to learn the following.

In music the first seven letters of the alphabet are used ABCDEFG and repeated again if necessary ABCDEFG ABCDE ... etc. In between most of them there are semitones or halftones called Sharps or Flats.

A Sharp (#) raises a note up a semitone and a Flat (♭) lowers a note down a semitone. (A semitone is the distance from one fret to another.)

Therefore A# would be the same as B♭

A (A#/B♭) B C (C#/D♭) D (D#/E♭) E F (F#/G♭) G (G#/A♭) A

Follow the diagrams carefully.

Finger on E chord:

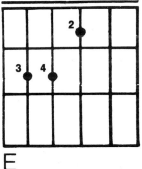

E

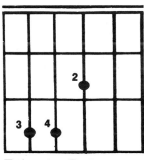

Take the E shape up a semitone (one fret)

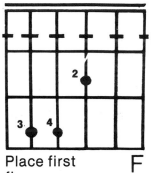

Place first finger over the first fret

F

If you bring (slide) your fingers up another semitone you would get F.

If you raise your fingers up another semitone you will get F#.

If you had started off with E7 or Em instead of E you would have got F7 or Fm etc. respectively in place of F.

As you can see by moving your fingers up along the fingerboard you can get many chords. Now try the A shape:

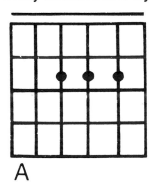

A

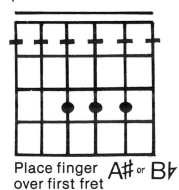

Place finger over first fret

A# or B♭

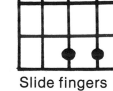

Slide fingers up another fret

B

If you slide this chord shape up another fret you will get C.

If you had started with A7 or Am you would have got B7 or Bm etc.